Once upon a time, a princess had a golden ball. It fell into a well.

A frog said, "I will get it for you, if you will promise to be my friend."

The princess promised.
So the frog got the ball.

But then the princess ran away.

At tea time, she heard a rat-a-tat-tat.

"Who is that?" said the king.

The princess told him all about the frog.

"I do not **want** to be friends with a smelly old frog!" she said.

The king was angry.

"If you make a promise, you must keep it," he said.

The princess had to let the frog have tea with her.

She had to take him to her bedroom.

The frog jumped up on to the bed. He looked sad.

The princess felt sorry for him. She stroked his head.

The frog turned into a prince!

"A witch put a spell on me," said the prince.

"Only the promise of a princess could break it," he said.

The prince and the princess fell in love.

They lived happily ever after.